Story of SCOTLAND

Book 1

Dorothy Morrison
and James Halliday

Oliver & Boyd

Contents

History Round About

All the stories in this book happened somewhere in Scotland. Every place has a history. You could learn quite a lot about the history of the place where you live. Perhaps something specially interesting happened in your district.

How can you find out?

1. Buildings

Look carefully at the older buildings near where you live. Do you see anything unusual – a date carved above a door, a roof, tiles, chimneys, windows, doorways?

In the countryside you may notice old walls, dovecots, ruined buildings and other signs of life long ago.

2. People

Other people may know. Older people are usually pleased to be asked if they can remember changes which have happened during their lifetime. They may be able to show you old photographs, postcards, notebooks or magazines.

3. The Library

Go to the library with your teacher and look at:

Books

Nearly every library has some books about the history of the district. They may be difficult to read or valuable, but ask the Librarian to help you. Some libraries and local tourist offices have booklets about their district's history.

Newspapers

Old local newspapers will tell you what went on in your district up to about 100 years ago. The library may have a copy of the local newspaper for a particular day you want to know about. Perhaps you and your teacher could have a look at it.

Maps

The Library may have old maps of your area which show how it has changed. Some libraries sell copies of these maps.

4. Place Names

Names of streets, houses, farms and fields can often tell you something about the past.

Blackfriars Street	Foundry Lane
Candleriggs	School Wynd
Grassmarket	West Port
Bow Butts	Nethergait
Castle Street	Jamaica Bridge
Limekilns	Trafalgar Street
Trongate	Bailie Street
Caithness Row	Links Park
Silk Street	Kitchener Street
Prestonpans	Saltcoats

5. Visit the Church

The minister will know the history of the building. Gravestones will tell you the names of the people who lived round about and, perhaps, the work they did.

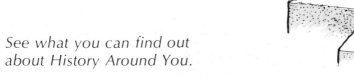

6. Visit the Museum

A local museum will have a great deal to show you about the past in your area. There may be pictures of local people or places.

See what you can find out about History Around You.

UNIT 1

Secret of the Sand

This story happened in 1850 in Orkney.
It is about the New Stone Age.

"Jimmie, I'm scared," whispered Mary. "Do you think the roof will blow off?"

"Of course not. Dinna be daft! But I wish that wind would stop. I canna get to sleep."

"Granny says there's never been a storm like this before. I think she's frightened too!"

The storm raged all night and part of the next day. In the houses round the Bay of Skaill the people huddled by their peat fires, and waited for the wind to die down. Sand was everywhere. It blew under the doors and through the cracks in the window frames.

"I hope the sand doesn't fill the whole house," thought Mary. Mary and Jimmie were glad to go out when the storm ended. Everywhere there were signs of the damage it had caused.

"There's the laird," said Jimmie. "What's he looking at over there on Skara Brae? Where did that great pile of stones come from?"

"Children, come over here," shouted Mr Watt, the laird. "Look, the sand has been hiding a secret. Now that the storm has blown the sand away we can see what was underneath."

"But it's just stones and rubbish," whispered Mary to her brother. "That's not much of a secret."

"Do you know what I think?" said Mr Watt. "We're looking at houses that were built thousands of years ago."

Mr Watt was right about the village he found at Skara Brae. The houses were built nearly 4 000 years ago. The people of Skara Brae then used well-made stone tools, but had nothing made of metal. Today the ruins are carefully looked after because they are New Stone Age houses.

The first picture shows some of the houses as they are today. There are no roofs now on the houses. The rafters were probably made of whalebone. They would be covered with skins and held up by a stone post. A hole in the middle would let out the smoke.

1. What are the houses made of?
2. Is the beach sandy or stony?

The people who lived at Skara Brae did not write anything down that could tell us about their way of life. To find out how they lived we must look at the clues they left behind.

A family lived in the one-room house in the next picture. The room is nearly 5 metres across.

3. Measure out 5 metres in your classroom.
4. Would the family have had a lot of living space?

In the centre of the hut there is a square of broken stone slabs. Inside this square peat ashes were found.

Near this fireplace there is a box shaped about 2 metres long and made of stone. It could have been filled with heather and dried grass.

The people in these houses would also need somewhere to keep food and other things.

5. Where is the fireplace?
6. Why are there large stones near the fireplace?
7. How might the stone shapes near the fire have been used?
8. Why might these houses get very smoky?
9. Draw the store-cupboard you can see in the picture. Put on the shelves what you think might have been put there.

This picture shows the doorway into the house. There were tunnels about 1 metre high between the houses.

10. Is the doorway large or small?
11. Would it be easy to walk in and out of a house?
12. What might you have to do?

Jimmie and Mary thought the ruined houses must have been built under the ground. But Mr Watt explained that they had been built above ground, and covered with a great mound of broken bones, ashes and shells. Mary thought this was a strange thing to do, but Jimmie thought he knew the reason.

"It's so cold and windy in Orkney in winter," he said. "If they piled up the rubbish outside it would help to keep the houses warm."

HOW THE SKARA BRAE FOLK BUILT THEIR HOUSES

1. They built their huts of stone with the doors facing each other.

2. They made their roofs of whalebone rafters covered with skin.

3. They piled rubbish round the outside walls.

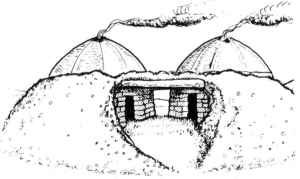

4. Last, they covered over the passageway with stone slabs and piled more rubbish on top.

13. Do you think it was a good idea to pile the rubbish up outside the houses?

14. Why might you not have liked having the rubbish outside your home?

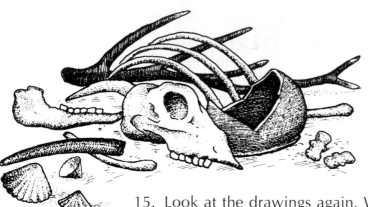

Here are some of the things found in the rubbish mounds.

Nearly everything at Skara Brae was made of stone. Very few trees grow in Orkney.

There were some cooking pots made of clay. Water and meat stews could be heated by putting hot stones in the clay pots.

15. Look at the drawings again. What do they suggest the people of Skara Brae had to eat?
16. What other things may they have had to eat?
17. One way of cooking has been suggested on this page. How else might meat be cooked?

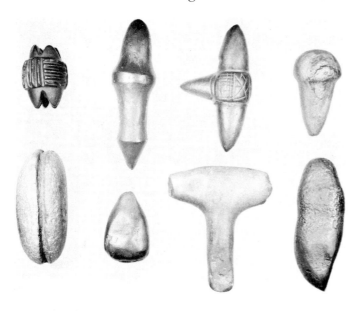

Mary wondered what kind of clothes the Skara Brae people wore. No clothes were found. But Mr Watt did find tools for scraping skins and pieces of flint and bone, or *borers*, which could make holes in skins. Look at the photograph to see what these tools were like.

18. Do you think it would take a long time to make these tools from a piece of stone?
19. Why do you think so?

When Mr Watt began to examine the village, the houses and passages were choked with sand. The people who lived there had left behind all their stores and many of their belongings.

Some of them must have taken a very long time to make. The people must have left in a hurry.

20. Why do you think the people of Skara Brae left their houses so quickly?

Perhaps a great sandstorm like the one that frightened Jimmie and Mary forced them to rush out of their homes. More and more sand would pile up until at last the houses were completely covered. For nearly 4 000 years no one knew the secret hidden in the sand.

Things to Do

Writing

The people of Skara Brae would be very pleased if a whale was stranded on the shore. They could use the meat for food,

the bones to make roof supports, scrapers, borers and needles,

the skin for clothes and roofing,
the blubber to make oil.

Write a story called *The Day the Great Whale was Stranded.*

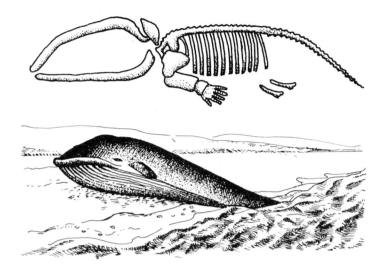

Drawing and Painting

1. Each person in the class could draw a picture of a tool used by the people at Skara Brae. Cut out the pictures carefully and stick them on a large piece of paper to make a wall chart. Head it *Tools used at Skara Brae.*

2. Draw and paint pictures to show
   a. Making stone tools at Skara Brae.
   b. Cleaning skins and stretching them out to dry.

Acting

Think of all the jobs the people at Skara Brae would have to do. Without speaking, act out one of these jobs in front of the class, and see if the others can guess what you are doing.

Making Models

1. Here is one way that people of the New Stone Age made pots.

   a. Rub wet clay between your hands and make a long snake.
   b. Wind the snake round and round. Put one ring on top of another until the pot is the size you wish.
   c. Smooth out the joins with your fingers.
   d. Decorate the pot by making marks with your nails or with a piece of bone or stick.

   You could try making a pot out of either clay or plasticine.

2. Make a room like one of the Skara Brae houses. You will need a pile of small stones and a box with no lid. Make stone furniture by sticking the stones with plasticine or Blu-Tack. Remember to have a fire-place, store-cupboard, beds and stones for sitting on. Cover the outside of the box with wet paper pulp mixed with some sand. Put some sand on the floor and dried grass in beds.

Places to Visit

Things which happened before the time when men could write are called *Prehistoric*. Are there any remains near your school of people of prehistoric times, e.g. earth houses, standing stones, stone circles, burial cairns?

People who search in places like this for clues about the past are called *Archaeologists*. See if you can visit one or find out anything about them to tell to the class.

If you live near a museum you could make drawings of any stone age tools, ornaments or weapons on display. Some may have been found near where you live. Write a sentence about each one and make a small book called *Stone Age Tools in the Museum*.

Books to read

A good story about life at Skara Brae is *The Boy with the Bronze Axe* by K. Fidler (Puffin, 1972). Another enjoyable story is *Shifting Sands* by R. Sutcliff (Hamilton, 1977).

Other books which tell more about life in prehistoric times are:

Prehistoric Britain by R. Place (Longman)
Stone Age Man in Britain (Ladybird)
The Story of Houses and Homes (Ladybird)
The Story of Archaeology by A. Allan (Faber)
Early Britain by B. Taylor and J. Bareham (*Picture Reference Books*, Brockhampton)
Prehistoric Britain by R. R. Sellman (Methuen).

A book which gives model cut-outs to make is *Stone Age Britain* by John Platts (*Active History*, Macmillan).

UNIT 2

The Sacred Island

This story happened in the year 563 AD on the island of
Iona off the rocky west coast of Scotland.

Neil was crouching in a hollow among the rocks. He
peered out into the storm. "Is the little dark shape I
saw earlier still there?" he wondered.

The young boy knew that the dangerous Torren
Rocks could tear a small boat to pieces. Then he gave a
sigh of relief. Bobbing up and down on the waves he
could see a little round boat, a *coracle*, with a group of
people on board. One of them was pointing towards
the cliff where he was hidden. Quietly Neil watched
them land in the deep bay below, and pull their coracle
on to the stony beach. They eagerly gathered round a
tall, fair man who seemed to be in charge.

The stranger shielded his eyes and gazed back over
the sea. He shook his head and set off up the cliff with
the others following behind. Neil followed too. The
men climbed to the top of the highest hill on the island.
Neil was curious, but he did not feel frightened.

Once again the strangers all gazed out to sea. This
time their leader took a stone and laid it carefully on the
ground. The others added stones to it until they had
made a little mound. Then they knelt down and bowed
their heads.

"What does this mean?" thought Neil. "Why are
these people here? Have they come to stay?"

The men Neil saw had come from Ireland. They had come to teach the people in Scotland about Jesus Christ. Their leader was Columba, a man of noble family. He had decided to leave his own country and serve Christ by teaching the Scots. Columba knew that the Scots had come from Ireland too. They spoke the same language and had many of the same customs.

The king of the Scots had been killed in battle by the Picts. They lived in the north of Scotland and spoke a different language. Columba hoped he might be able to help the Scots, and make the Picts good Christians.

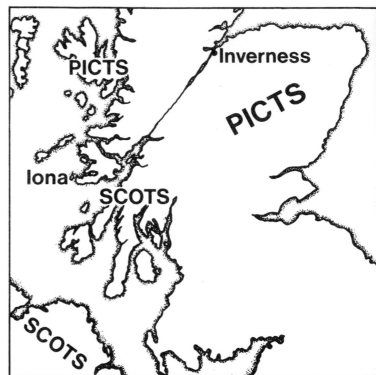

Columba was sad to leave his home. Neil watched him climb the highest hill on Iona.

1. Why do you think Columba wanted to make sure he could no longer see Ireland from the island?
2. Would it be easier for Columba to teach the Scots or the Picts? Say why.

This is a coracle, the type of boat in which Columba sailed. It is made of branches and covered with skins.

3. From the box choose the words which you think best describe the coracle.
4. Say why you think so.

HEAVY	SMALL	AWKWARD
SAFE	LIGHT	STRONG

Columba and his friends were monks. They had made special promises:

> They would own nothing for themselves.
> They would never marry.
> They would be kind to all travellers and those in need.
> They would always obey their leader.

Columba and his friends built a new home for themselves. We know what it looked like because a monk who lived on Iona after Columba wrote about it.

The most important building was the wooden church which had a bronze bell. Near the church were little huts made of wood and clay. They were shaped like bee-hives. The monks lived in them and slept on beds of heather covered with seal skins.

Columba's hut was built a little higher than the others beside a stream.

There were other little huts where visitors could stay. There was a dining place with a large stone for a table. This room had a fireplace.

Look at the picture.

5. Which building is the church?
6. How do you know?
7. Why might the monks need to protect their home?
8. Iona is very cold in winter. Where might the monks go to be warm?

Each monk wore a long shirt and on top a gown with a hood made of rough wool. They had leather sandals and an extra woollen cloak to wear in bad weather. The hair on the top of a monk's head was shaved. This hair-style was called a *tonsure*. All the monks went to church six times a day to pray and sing, but they also had to work hard at other jobs.

9. Would the monks' clothes be comfortable to wear all the year round? (Think about hot weather, rain, snow, cold.)
10. Unscramble these jumbled letters to find out some of the jobs the monks had to do.

LOPUHG   **WOS**   **KABE**   **LIMK**   **UBILD**   **SHIF**

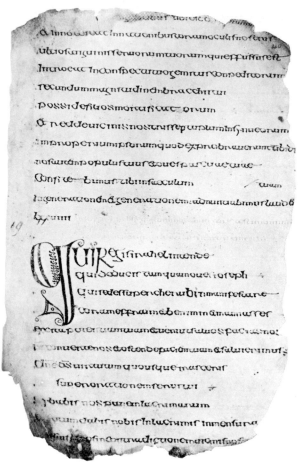

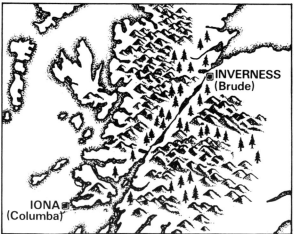

Some monks did not work in this way. They wrote out beautiful copies of books of the Bible or of the Psalms. This picture shows part of one of these books. It may have been written by Columba himself. There were no printing presses. All books had to be written by hand. There was no paper. They used parchment, which was made from the skin of a goat. Later, handwritten books were decorated with designs and pictures.

11. Why would books be very precious things to own?

One important job for monks was to go to many other parts of the country to teach people about Jesus Christ.

After he had been two years on Iona, Columba went with some of the other monks on a long, hard journey. He wanted to visit the King of the Picts, who was called Brude. King Brude lived near the place where Inverness is now.

12. Why do you think Columba waited for two years before he went to the Picts?
13. Look carefully at the map. What do you think would be the best way for Columba to travel? (Remember, there were no proper roads, but thick dark forests and high mountains.)
14. Suggest some of the difficulties Columba might face on the journey.

Columba's visit was a success. Brude and his people listened to what he had to say. They decided to become Christians. Many strange stories were told of great wonders happening when Columba was present. For example, people claimed that the great gates of Brude's palace opened themselves when Columba made the sign of the cross.

The Picts and Scots were now Christians. They became more friendly, for both peoples felt that Iona was a special, holy place. Much later, in 843, Kenneth MacAlpin, King of the Scots, became King of the Picts as well.

The Picts made beautiful decorated carvings on stone. Sometimes these were finely carved crosses which might have marked a special sacred place.

This is what Columba wrote about Iona. "Although this is only a small island, people will honour it some day, not only the Scots and their kings, but people from other countries too."

He was right!

There is still a church on Iona.

The photograph shows the abbey which was built long after the time of Columba. The buildings had become ruins but a group of people have worked hard for many years to build them up again as you see.

Today Iona is visited by thousands of visitors each year from all over the world. They come to see the Sacred Island where Columba and his followers settled.

Things to Do

Writing

Imagine you are the boy, Neil, who watched Columba and his friends arrive on Iona. Write down what he might say to his family about the newcomers. Mention their boat, their clothes, what they did.

Drawing and Painting

1. Each person in the class could draw a picture of a monk at work, e.g. fishing, digging, milking, writing. Try to make all the monks the same size. Cut them out carefully and stick them on a large piece of paper to make a wall chart.
   Make a heading – **MONKS ON IONA.**
2. On a large piece of paper draw a standing stone like those made by the Picts. Decorate it with symbols like the ones on page 15.

Acting

A group of monks have been sent by Columba to preach to a fierce tribe of people living far away from Iona. He has given them a cross to carry with them. The monks must go, because they have made a promise to obey. They are afraid of the journey and of how the people will treat them. Act out what they might say to each other on the way and what happens when they arrive.

Places to Visit

There may be places near your school where there was once an early Christian church or sacred place, e.g. Aberdour, Turriff, Abercorn, Whithorn, Govan had settlements like the one on Iona. Perhaps you live near some of the three hundred or so carved Pictish stones or your local museum may have one. See if you can visit or find out anything about them to tell the class.

Something to Talk About

Do you think these monks had an easy life?

Books to Read

Perhaps you might like to find out what life was like in later monasteries. Here are some books you might like to look at:

The Medieval Monastery by M. Reeves (Longman, Then & There)
A Northumbrian Missionary (OUP, People of the Past)
A Children's Book of Scottish Saints by A. M. D. Henderson-Howat (Harrap).
A book which tells of wars between the Picts and the Scots in the time of St Columba is The Eaglet and the Angry Dove by J. Oliver (Macmillan).
The Mark of the Horselord by R. Sutcliff (OUP) tells of the fighting between the Scots in the sixth century.

UNIT 3

The Bridge and the Castle

This story happened at Stirling Bridge in September 1297

The Earl of Surrey looked round at his huge English army. Then he pointed to the castle of Stirling high up on its rock. "It is just good luck," he said, "that the Scots have taken so many castles back from their English masters. But they must not take Stirling. This bridge across the River Forth is the main way to get from the north of Scotland to the south." Surrey was sure he could deal with this outlaw Scot, William Wallace, and his mob on the other side of the bridge. After all, Wallace was not even a noble!

"Let us cross the bridge and attack now," said Treasurer Cressingham. "Don't waste time sending men to the ford up the river."

Friar Cuthbert and his friend did not feel so sure. There were so many stories of Wallace's courage. They knew he hated the English invaders who had killed his wife and burned his home.

"Perhaps he has damaged the bridge so that it will give way when we cross," replied Surrey. Suddenly he turned to the two friars. "We'll give the cowards a chance," he said. "You will cross the bridge and tell the robber, Wallace, he may have a pardon if he gives in."

Cuthbert and his friend walked slowly across the narrow bridge, tightly clutching the wooden crosses which hung from ropes at their waists.

The tall, fair-haired Wallace laughed loudly when they gave their message. "Go back!" he shouted so that all his men could hear. "Tell your master we did not come for peace. We fight for our freedom."

The great seal of Edward I

Edward I, King of England, had conquered Wales. He wanted to rule Scotland as well. He thought the two countries should be joined to make one strong country. Then there would be no danger of England being invaded from the north. The Scots could not then be friendly with countries which were enemies of England.

At first he tried to do this without going to war. When he failed he invaded Scotland and took away many treasures.

He put English soldiers in all the important Scottish castles. The Earl of Surrey, an Englishman, was put in charge of all Scotland. Another Englishman, Hugh of Cressingham, looked after the money of Scotland and collected the taxes.

1. Why do you think Edward I was called 'The Hammer of the Scots'?
2. Do you think the Scots would like to see Englishmen everywhere behaving as if they were masters of Scotland?
3. What might they try to do?

The Coronation Chair with the Stone of Destiny underneath the seat

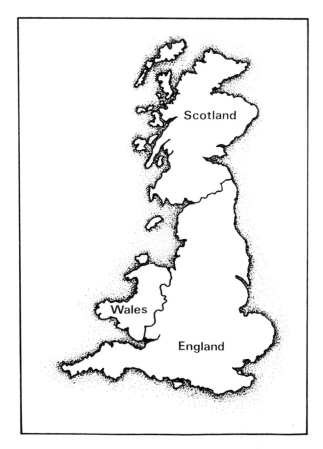

William Wallace owned land at Elderslie, near Paisley. He gathered men together to help him drive the English out of Scotland. At first, he and his friends attacked small towns and castles where there were not too many English soldiers.

They managed to capture many castles. Other Scotsmen tried to do the same and soon Edward began to worry that the English might be driven out of Scotland.

This statue of William Wallace is on the wall of Edinburgh Castle

A large English army led by the Earl of Surrey was sent to Stirling to deal with Wallace. Surrey had many more troops than Wallace. They were all well-armed and used to fighting in battle. He had many knights on horseback too.

Wallace's men were not used to fighting in great battles. They had far fewer weapons and not many men on horseback.

4. Which side would you expect to win the battle?

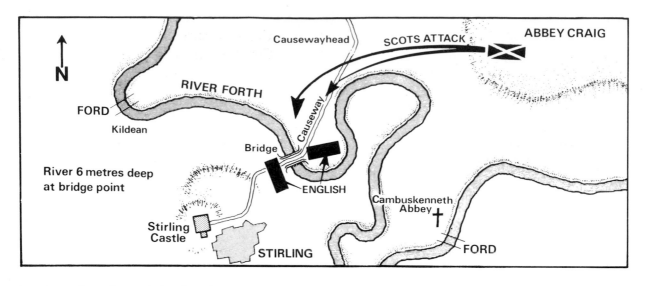

Look at the plan of the battle.

The English army had to cross the River Forth to reach the Scots. The River Forth at Stirling was very deep, but there was a ford further up where sixty people could cross at a time. The bridge was only wide enough for two men to walk side by side.

5. Where were Wallace and his men at the start?

6. Would it be easy for a large army to cross the bridge quickly? Say why not.

7. What might happen to the English soldiers if they crossed the bridge?

8. How else might they cross the river?

When Friar Cuthbert and his friend came back across the bridge and told the English leaders that Wallace would not give in, the Earl of Surrey had to decide what to do. People had different ideas.

A Knight's Plan	Cressingham's Plan
Send 500 knights and some soldiers to cross the ford. They can attack Wallace's men from behind while the rest are crossing the river.	Cross the bridge as quickly as possible. To use the ford is a waste of time and the King's money.

9. Which plan do you think was better? Say why.

Surrey took Cressingham's advice. The English began to cross the bridge two by two.

Wallace let many of them cross the bridge, and then his spearmen rushed down and captured the end of the bridge so that no one else could get through. The bridge was crowded with men and horses. As more soldiers crowded on to the bridge, people pressed backwards and forwards. The bridge began to collapse. The picture shows what happened.

Wallace and his men won a great victory at Stirling Bridge.

Later Wallace was captured and killed. The famous Robert Bruce became Scotland's king. All the castles were freed from the English soldiers and the Scots ruled their own country.

This picture of the Battle of Stirling Bridge was painted early this century by William Hole.

Things to Do

Writing

Friar Cuthbert managed to escape after the battle at Stirling Bridge. Write his story of what happened as he tells it to another friar. Remember to mention the Earl of Surrey, Cressingham, the narrow bridge, the ford, what the soldiers looked like, Wallace's plan.

Drawing and Painting

Make a picture strip of:

1. Surrey telling Friar Cuthbert and his friend to take a message to Wallace.
2. The two frightened friars crossing the bridge.
3. Wallace telling the friars he will never give in.

Acting

When Edward I heard about Stirling Bridge he would not be very pleased! Make a class play of what happens when a soldier arrives to tell Edward the news. As well as the soldier you will need people to act as Edward, a herald to announce the soldier, several lords and knights and other servants.

Something to Talk About

Do you think the Earl of Surrey was a good soldier?

If you had been an Englishman would you have thought Edward I was right to invade Scotland?

Not all Scotsmen fought for Wallace or Bruce. What would you have done? Say why.

Places to Visit

1. If you do not live too far from Stirling it might be possible for you to visit the Wallace monument and Stirling Castle.
2. Those who live in the north of Scotland might like to find out about Andrew de Murray who also fought against the English. His castle was at Avoch, near Inverness.
3. The National Trust Site at Bannockburn, near Stirling, has a film which shows how Bruce won a great victory at Bannockburn.

Books to Read

Some books which will tell you more about this time are:

Tales of King Robert the Bruce by T. Scott (Pergamon)
King Robert the Bruce by Margaret J. Miller (MacDonald)
How they lived in the Age of Knights by S. Hademus and B. Jaurup (Lutterworth)
Scotland in the Time of Wallace and Bruce by W. K. Ritchie (Longman, *Then and There*).

UNIT 4

Dusty Feet

This story happened in Montrose in the fifteenth century

It was almost sunset. Adam Dickie, the travelling merchant, hurried along the dusty road leading to Montrose. His old horse, Mirrem, plodded on slowly. The cloth she carried on her back was very heavy. Robin, Adam's son, prodded her with a pointed stick.

"Come on Mirrem!" he shouted. "We must get there before the gates close or we won't be able to sell anything at the fair tomorrow."

At the town gates a crowd of people waited to go through. The town officers looked at each person carefully and asked what they had come to sell. They were only allowed in after they had paid a tax.

Robin looked all round about him as he walked up the High Street towards the Mercat Cross. Merchants and their wives, knights, herdsmen, soldiers, friars, fishwives, beggars, craftsmen, sailors and pedlars crowded the town. Everyone seemed very busy setting up booths and stalls for the fair which would open the next day. Apprentices (young boys who were learning a trade) were shutting up their masters' shops, for they would stay closed during the fair. At the inn a stable boy took Mirrem to the stables at the back.

"We've been given a good place near the tron," said Adam. "We should sell our stock of cloth easily."

But Robin was not listening. "Look father," he cried. "There's a huge, hairy monster walking down the street!"

The fair was held every year in July. It was an important time in Montrose. Everyone for miles round about travelled in to buy and sell and have a good time. Merchants who had travelled along the dusty roads, like Adam Dickie, were called Dusty Feet.

Adam's stall was beside the tron. It was a big beam balance and all the goods were weighed on it.

Some of the stalls had signs to show what was for sale.

The Town Officers tested all the bread, wine and ale to see that it was of good quality.

Adam had come to sell cloth.

1. How many other things can you see for sale in the top picture?
2. Why would Adam think his stall was in a good place?
3. Why might it be a good idea to check the weights of the food and other things which were sold?
4. Look for the signs of the shoemaker, the butcher and the chemist. What other signs can you see on this page?

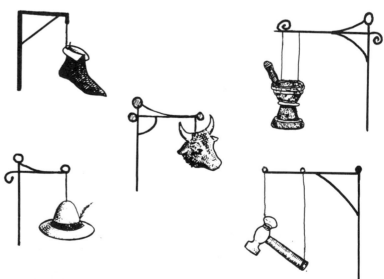

Adam and Robin had a busy day. They sold nearly as much as at the market in Aberdeen. They sold blue linen to the wife of the town bailie. A wealthy knight bought embroidered silk for his lady.

Robin was watching Adam measuring out fine woollen cloth for a rich merchant. Suddenly, he noticed a sly-looking man, who had been standing close by, move off quickly into the crowd. The next instant the merchant was clutching the cord at his waist. His leather purse had been stolen!

   "A cut-purse!" he cried. "Stop thief!" Too late. The thief had disappeared.

5. Why would it be easy for the thief to escape?

The stalls were set up round about the *mercat* (market) *cross*. This was where the town crier stood when he had something important to tell the townspeople.

   Look at the lower picture.

6. What is the town crier holding in his right hand?
7. Why would he need it?

There were always amusements at a fair. The big, hairy monster which Robin was so surprised to see was a dancing bear.

This picture shows other amusements at the fair. Near the cloth-stall there is a hurdy-gurdy player. One man is playing the flute for the acrobats.

8. What other musicians can you see in the picture?
9. How many plates is the juggler trying to keep in the air?
10. Where might you go to see acts like these today?

One thing Robin did enjoy. There was always plenty to eat at a fair. As well as the stalls selling bread and pies, there would be others with hot soup, smoked hams, geese, chickens, eggs, salt fish, onions or cheese. Rich merchants might buy wine brought from abroad, but there was always home-brewed ale or milk to drink too.

Adam gave Robin a penny to buy some spices for his mother. These could help to make salt meat taste a little better. In winter time salt meat was all you could get.

11. Why do you think this was?
12. Can you rearrange the jumbled letters to find the spices Robin bought?

nnicaonm

nigreg

tungem

locves

26

Robin took a walk down by the harbour to look at the ships. He could see a wine ship from France. Montrose was a busy port. Piled up for loading were barrels of salted salmon, salted herrings and dried cod.

Sometimes hides and animal skins were sent abroad also. Other ports sent wool or furs.

13. Why would the fish be salted or dried?
14. How is fish kept fresh today?

As Robin walked back up the Seagate past the wooden houses with their thatched roofs, he noticed that some houses were charred and black. Their roofs had disappeared. He knew what must have happened – fire. He remembered his father telling him that once the whole town of Montrose had gone on fire.

15. Why would it be easy for the fire to spread quickly?

Robin hurried on for he knew his father would be angry if he stayed away too long.

"All the same," he thought. "A fair only comes once a year. I might as well enjoy myself."

Things to Do

Writing

Read the story again and look at the picture on page 24. Make a list of as many different kinds of people as you can who might be at a fair.

Acting

Pretend you are a stallholder at the fair. Act out to the rest of the class what you might say to coax people to buy your goods, e.g. cloth, meat, hides, sheepskins, eggs, knives and so on.

Places to Visit

This map shows other towns in Scotland in the fifteenth century which would have held fairs. Do you live near one? Does your town have a mercat cross, a High Street, a Market Street or a Trongate?

Something to Talk About

People enjoyed the fair because it was a holiday for them. Many towns still have their own fair holiday. The Glasgow Fair is always the second two weeks of July, and most Glasgow people still go on holiday at this time.

Does your town have its own Fair Holiday time?

Books to Read

A good story about life at this time is *The Armourer's House* by R. Sutcliff (OUP 1962).

To find out more about town life you might look at:

Medieval Life by V. Bailey & E. Wise (Longman 1968)
Markets and Fairs by Jane Dorner (Wayland, 1975)
Town Life in the Middle Ages by P. Davis (Wayland, 1975)
Medieval Times by John Shepherd (*Picture Panorama*, Owlet, 1977).

UNIT 5

Long Live the King!

This story happened in Edinburgh on 26th March 1603

It was late on Saturday night and the courtiers of King James VI were very tired. They could not go to bed for the king was still awake. He sat in the room outside his bedroom looking anxious and excited.

Suddenly there was a shout and a noise of hurrying feet. Through the door came a strange sight. The Englishman, Sir Robert Carey, almost fell into the room. His clothes were covered in mud. There was a large red mark on the side of his face, and blood ran from a cut above his eye.

Everyone stopped talking as he made his way towards the king and knelt down before him.

"Your Majesty," he gasped. "Your cousin Elizabeth, Queen of England, is dead. You are now King of England as well as Scotland."

"Long live the King!" shouted everyone at once.

James sat back and looked at them all. He hardly knew what to say. For years he had thought about this moment. Now a Stuart was King of England! He would be king of a much larger country than Scotland. He would have much more money and power. Of course, he would have to live in England. He would have to live among people who spoke in a different way and went to a different kind of church, but this did not make him sad. He had not always been happy in Scotland. Too many people thought they knew better than the king how to rule. In England he would allow no one to tell him what to do.

"I shall try to be a good king," he said.

James VI became king of Scotland when he was less than one year old. His mother, Mary Queen of Scots, had not been liked by some important nobles in Scotland. She was forced to give up being queen. James could not remember seeing her at all.

James VI as a young boy

Some of the nobles were very keen to look after James while he was growing up. This would give them great power in Scotland. They would tell the king what to do. He was moved around from the house of one lord to another. He was sometimes afraid he might be killed. In 1582 he was kidnapped by the Ruthven family.

At last, when he was 17, James decided he was able to rule by himself. He escaped from the Ruthvens and chose clever men to work for him. He gave them money and made them lords if they served him loyally.

Queen Elizabeth of England ruled a much larger country. Her court was rich and powerful.

She reigned for 45 years, but she had no children. James VI was her nearest relation.

Queen Elizabeth of England on her way to Blackfriars with her courtiers

1. Do you think James VI had a very happy childhood? Say why.
2. Why would James wish to rule England?

As soon as Sir Robert Carey brought the news that Elizabeth was dead, James began to get ready for moving to London. He wished to look like a great king, so he ordered special suits of clothes. They were made of silk and velvet, and trimmed with fur, braid and jewels. He had a splendid carriage and fine horses. A great number of courtiers travelled with him when he set out on 5th April.

"There was great crying and grieving among the ordinary people for the loss of the daily sight of their King," one writer tells us.

3. Why did the people of Edinburgh feel so sad when James left?

At Berwick the king was shown round the great walls of the town. The soldiers on duty were surprised that he was so friendly and pleasant. He even tried firing one of the big guns for fun.

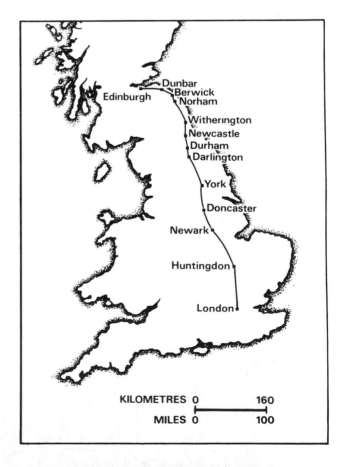

James VI's route to London

The important people of every shire came riding out to meet him. Great crowds of people cheered and waved as he passed through their towns. He heard long speeches of welcome. He was given rich gifts.

James looked at the rich green countryside as he rode along and thought, "This is my country. I am the ruler of all these people."

Later he told a friend, "The first time I came into this kingdom the people of all sorts rode and ran, in fact rushed to meet me."

James was so pleased that he gave special titles and gifts to many of the people who came to see him.

At least 300 people were made knights. But at last the crowds became so great that the king had to ask that no more should come to meet him.

4. Why do you think so many people wished to see the new king?
5. Why might James grow tired of this?

James would have liked to make a grand entry into London, but a terrible sickness called plague was killing many people. The disease spread quickly in the towns. No one knew how to cure the plague.

People thought plague was in the air. They carried posies of sweet-smelling herbs and flowers when they had to walk through the streets. They thought these little bunches of flowers might help to keep the plague away.

A ring, a ring of roses
A pocket full of posies
A tishoo. A tishoo
We all fall down!

This nursery rhyme describes what happened to people with plague.

King James spent two months living just outside London. Even when he was crowned king at Westminster Abbey at the end of July only a small number of people were there.

6. Why would it be wise to avoid a crowded place at this time?
7. Why were so few people there to see James being crowned king?

Scotland's king now lived in England. He stayed in London and wrote letters to his councillors in Scotland telling them what to do.

8. Would it be easy for Scottish people to see their king?
9. How would the king find out what was happening in Scotland?
10. Do you think the Scottish people would like this new arrangement?
11. What might they say?

The next story tells what happened when James came back to visit Scotland in 1617.

Wax statue of James VI

Things to Do

Writing
1. Imagine you are in Edinburgh on the day King James VI leaves for his new kingdom of England. Describe the splendid procession, mentioning how the king is dressed, his carriage and horses and what the people around you are saying.
2. Make up the verses of a song about the king leaving Scotland to the tune of *Polly put the Kettle On*

   e.g. Our King has gone to England now
   Our King has gone to England now
   Our King has gone to England now
   We all feel sad.

Acting
Make a class play about Sir Robert Carey telling James he is king of England.

Drawing and Painting
Draw and colour a picture-strip showing:
1. Sir Robert Carey telling James he is king of England.
2. James in his splendid new clothes.
3. The king on the great walls at Berwick.
4. People carrying posies to keep the plague away.

Mapping
On a map of Britain mark the journey of James from Edinburgh to London. Mark the Border. How did James travel? How might this journey be made today?

Places to Visit
1. The National Portrait Gallery in Edinburgh has interesting paintings of James VI and other Stuart rulers.
2. Provand's Lordship in Glasgow was visited by James's mother, Mary Queen of Scots.
3. John Knox's House and Gladstone's Land in Edinburgh are the kind of houses the better-off people might have lived in when James was king.

Books to Read
An exciting story which tells about spies in sixteenth-century Edinburgh is *The Spanish Letters* by M. Hunter (Puffin, 1972).

UNIT 6

The King gets a Fright

*This story happened in the early 17th century
in Culross in Fife*

Sir George Bruce, the richest man in Culross, felt very proud as he stepped forward to greet his visitors. "Welcome, your Majesty," he said, bowing low.

King James VI was paying his first visit to Scotland since he had gone to London as King of England 14 years before.

"Sir George," said the king, "I have heard much talk of your wonderful coal mines. I am told they run for more than a mile under the sea. While men are busy digging coal many ships are sailing overhead. Men say that you can go into the mine from the land and from the sea. Tell me, how is it possible to keep the sea water out of the mine?"

Sir George explained that the entrance to the mine was on a sandbank, which was not covered with water at low-tide. He had made a great round stone wall so high and strong that the sea could not cover it.

"I must see this for myself," said the king.

He followed Sir George down the shaft. It was dark and dismal down below. The only light came from the flickering candles. Most of the time the King could walk upright. But where the roof was low he had to bend down so that he did not bump his head. He could hear the steady drip of water and the tapping of hammers and pickaxes. He looked along narrow passages, and saw miners with black faces and bodies. Only the whites of their eyes shone in the dark.

At last, he saw a gleam of light ahead. They had reached the end of the mine. He was glad to be pulled up the shaft to go above ground again.

What a shock he got! They had arrived at the sea entrance at high tide. He was surrounded by water!

"Help!" he cried. "It's a plot to kill me."

Sir George Bruce's house
(The Palace) at Culross today

Sir George Bruce was a rich merchant in Culross, in Fife. He had a fine new house built for him. It was started in 1597.

The roof was made of red tiles. The walls inside were lined with pine wood panels. There were splendid painted ceilings, made of wood.

The pictures on the ceilings and on the walls were copied from a book of paintings. One bedroom had a rising sun painted on one wall, and a setting sun on another.

1. The drawing shows part of another ceiling. The words at the top are in Latin. Can you read the words underneath? What do they say?

OMNIS CARO FOENUM

All flesche is grasse, and withereth lyke the haye
And warneth us how weill to live, but not how long to waye

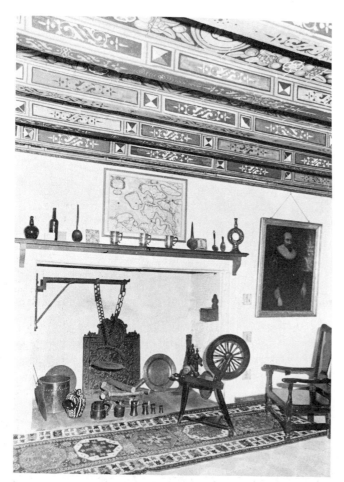

2. Why do you think only a few houses had ceilings like this?
3. What furniture can you see in this picture of a room?
4. Do you think the chairs would be comfortable to sit in?
5. What do you think was used for heating this house?

There was something unusual about the windows of Sir George's new house. Here is a drawing of one. It shows that only the top half of the window had glass.

6. Are the panes of glass large or small?
7. Why do you think this is?
8. What shape are the panes?
9. The bottom half has two doors called *shutters*. What do you think the shutters are made of?
10. What would they shut out?
11. Would you like this type of window in your house? Say why.

Above one of the windows Sir George had a fine carving made. You can see a shield in the centre.

12. What is the design on the shield?
13. What do the initials G B stand for?
14. Why has the date 1597 been carved?

Sir George Bruce made money for himself and the people of Culross by making salt from sea water and by mining coal. He owned ships which could tie up in the deep water at the mine shaft to take on coal. Over 100 tonnes of coal was sent abroad every week.

The next picture shows how the salt was probably made.

We know that the sea water was dried in large iron pans heated with coal. These were called salt pans.

It was very hard to keep food fresh in Sir George's time. People used a lot of salt for this.

15. Suggest why a place like this might be called 'The Pans'.
16. What must have been made at the towns of Saltcoats and Prestonpans?

Sir George Bruce's ships brought back iron from Sweden to Culross.
Iron was used to make many things. But the people of Culross had
the special right to make the iron girdles on which scones and
oatcakes could be cooked.

Nearly every family in Scotland would have a girdle for baking.

Look at the map.

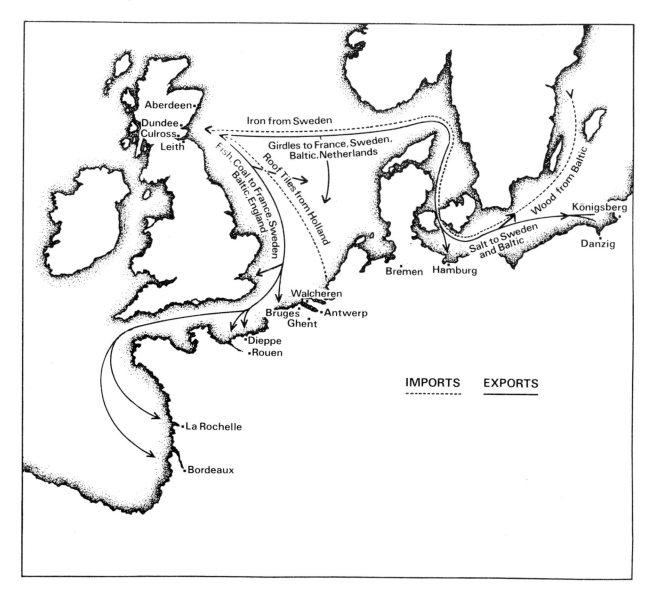

17. To which countries did the Culross
    ships go?
18. What were the goods which Sir
    George Bruce and the people of
    Culross sent abroad?
19. What goods were sent back to
    Culross?
20. From which country might Sir George
    have got the red tiles for the roof of
    his new house?

Visitors came to Culross to see the machine for pumping water out of the mine. A visitor drew pictures of the clever way the mine was drained by a long line of 36 buckets pulled by horses.

Sir George felt sure that there was no danger of the sea water coming in to the mine. But in 1625 there was a very high tide, and a great storm raged all along the east coast of Scotland. A writer tells us that:

"the like of this tempest was not seen in our time nor the like of it heard of in Scotland before. Saltpans were thrown down, ships and boats broken and the coalmines beside Culross were drowned."

21. How do we know that this storm was worse than usual winter storms?
22. What happened to the saltpans and coalmines at Culross?
23. What would happen to the people working in the mines?
24. How would Sir George feel as he watched the great storm?
25. Would he be able to carry on his business easily? Say why.

This disaster made Sir George very sad. He became ill and a few months later he died. Culross had lost its great merchant, but his house and the town which he knew are still there to visit today.

Things to Do

Writing

You are a reporter writing a newspaper story of what happened in Culross when the great storm came in 1625. Describe the storm, the damage it caused and your talk afterwards with Sir George Bruce.

Drawing and Painting

1. Draw a picture of the king in the mine.
2. Make designs for a painted ceiling for your house.
3. Paint a picture of the great storm flooding the mine.

Acting

1. Make a play of the story about the king in the mine and act it in class.
2. Pretend you are Sir George Bruce showing a group of people round his new house. One person should be Sir George walking from room to room and pointing things out. The others could be visitors who ask questions.

Something to Talk About

Culross still looks like a town in the sixteenth century. When we are there we can see what other Scottish towns must have looked like long ago. A lot of money has been spent on making the houses modern inside, but they have not been made modern on the outside.

Do you think it is a good idea to spend money on old buildings like this?

Would it be better to knock these old houses down and build new ones?

Places to Visit

Many other towns, besides Culross, still have old houses and streets. You might visit an old building in your town or try to collect street names which tell about the past of the town.

Something to Read

You can find out more about the mines at Culross in *Scotland in the Days of James VI* by Hyman Shapiro (*Then & There*, Longman). An adventure story about Culross in 1625 is *Escape in Darkness* by Kathleen Fidler (Lutterworth, 1961).

The Provost
who had to hide

This story happened in Glasgow in 1707

The Provost of Glasgow was a very important man. He was head of the council which ran the city. People would step out of his way to allow him to pass. They would admire the smart red cloak which he wore.

One day he found things were different. He was walking towards the fine house where he lived, when he noticed a large, noisy crowd of people gathered in the street. "There he is," someone shouted. "It's his fault! He's for the Union. He wouldn't send the message to parliament."

The crowd rushed towards the Provost. He tried to hurry up the street, but was pushed and jostled.

"We don't want to join the English!" a man screamed.

"You're trying to give our country away," another shouted. "They'll make us pay heavy taxes and we'll have to do what the English want."

Some small boys picked up stones and began to throw them. A large lump of mud hit the Provost on the nose, and a well aimed stone knocked off his hat.

"I must get away from this," he thought in panic. He ran into a close, up the stairs and into a house on the left-hand side. "Hide me, please," he begged.

The crowd followed close behind, but they pushed into the house on the other side of the stair. "He's not here!" cried a man. "Search the whole building!"

Although the crowd went through every room, they did not find the Provost. He lay shaking with fear inside a bed which folded up against the wall.

The reason the Glasgow crowd was so angry with the Provost was that he believed that Scotland and England should join together in a Union to make one country.

The ruler of both Scotland and England at this time was Queen Anne. She knew it was very hard to rule two different countries at once. Sometimes what suited one country did not suit the other. Think what would happen in a war if England fought against a country which was friendly with Scotland. Queen Anne thought that it would be good for both Scotland and England if they joined together and had only one parliament between them.

SCOTLAND's
Great Advantages
BY AN
UNION with ENGLAND:
Shown in a
LETTER
From the
COUNTRY,
To a Member of
PARLIAMENT.

By Iralon of philicoddan

Printed in the Year MDCCVI.

Lawful *Prejudices* against
an Incorporating
UNION
with *England*;
O R,
Some modest CONSIDERATIONS
ON
The sinfulness of this *UNION*, and the
Danger flowing from it to the
Church of *SCOTLAND*.

Ezra ch: 9. v: 13, 14. *And after all this is come upon us for our evil deeds, and for our great trespass, seing that thou our God hast punished us less than our iniquities deserve, and hast given us such a deliverance as this : Should we again break thy commandments, and joyn in Affinity with the people of these abominations? wouldest not thou be angry with us till thou hadst consumed us, so that there should be no remnant nor escaping?* Isaiah ch. 8. v. 12. *Say ye not, A confederacy to all them to whom this people shall say, A confederacy; neither fear ye their fear, nor be afraid.*

EDINBURGH, printed in the year 1707.

1. These pamphlets were written about the Union. Which was for and which against?
2. Read the arguments on the next page carefully and decide which ones might have been made by:
   a. A merchant who traded with other countries.
   b. A lawyer who thought Scots law was best.
   c. A church minister who did not want changes made in the church of Scotland.

Parliament House,
Edinburgh, today

The parliament of Scotland met in Edinburgh to decide what to do.
Here are some of the arguments which people made.

1. We need to sell the things we make to England. If we don't join, they won't buy our goods.	8. Scotland is a poor country. England will give us money from their taxes to help us become richer.
2. England might attack us if we don't join. They have a bigger army.	9. Scots will have to pay English taxes and they are higher.
3. England would not really attack us. We should not join.	10. England has land abroad and can make a lot of money through trade. We could do the same if we joined them.
4. Because England is bigger than Scotland more attention will be paid to what England wants.	11. The English will try to make us just like them and we are different.
5. Both Scotland and England have had the same king or queen since 1603. Why can't we have the same Parliament as well?	12. As long as the English don't try to change our laws it would be quite safe to join.
6. Ordinary Scottish people do not want to join with England.	13. Scotland has its own special church which is quite different from the Church of England. Unless our church is left alone we should not join.
7. If all our rulers are down in England, we Scots won't be able to keep an eye on what they are doing.	

When the parliament met in Edinburgh in 1707 to decide, 110 people voted for Union with England and 69 voted against it. It was decided that the people of Scotland, England and Wales should have one parliament. There was now one country – The United Kingdom of Great Britain.

Queen Anne
receiving the agreement
which joined
Scotland and England

In England most people were glad about the Union. They thought it would bring peace and friendship between the two countries. But in Scotland many people felt very sad. There were noisy meetings like the one in Glasgow where crowds showed how angry they were.

3. Why do you think Scots people might feel sad?
4. These are some of the things which changed after 1707:

Coins

Weights and Measures

The Army and Navy Taxes

Why was it thought better to have these the same for the whole of Britain?

The Scots did not want to change everything. So today they still have their own kind of:

Church

Schools

Laws

Banknotes

To show that Britain was now a United Kingdom, a new flag was made. It took the flag of Scotland, the cross of St Andrew, called the *Saltire*,

and the flag of England, the cross of St George, and joined them to make a new Union flag.

England and Scotland were now supposed to vanish and English and Scottish people were expected to think of themselves as *British*.

5. Has this happened?
6. How is the Union flag made in 1707 different from the Union Jack we know today?

Things to Do

Writing

The Provost of Glasgow must have been very frightened and angry when he was chased by the crowd. Write the letter he might have sent to a newspaper complaining about the way Glasgow people had treated him.

Drawing and Painting

1. Draw a picture-strip of the Provost
   a. Coming out of the Tolbooth
   b. Being chased by the crowd
   c. Losing his hat
   d. Asking for help in the house
   e. Hiding in the bed.
   Write what is happening underneath each picture.

2. Draw three shapes 8 cm by 5 cm. Make one the flag of Scotland – St Andrew's flag. Make the second the flag of England – St George's flag. In the third draw the union flag which was made in 1707.

Acting

1. Make a class play of the story about the Glasgow Provost.

2. a. Make one side of the classroom the place where supporters of the Union of Scotland and England meet. The other side is for those who are against the Union.
   b. Look at the arguments for and against the Union on page 43. Each person or group in the class should take a different argument.
   c. Have a discussion about joining Scotland and England. Make a speech beginning "I am for" (or "I am against") "the Union because . . ." and then stand at the side of the room where your argument belongs.

Something to Talk About

Many Scottish people speak differently from English people. Do you think there are other differences between Scotland and England today?

Places to Visit

There are many interesting places to visit in Edinburgh, the capital of Scotland:

The Law Courts.
Parliament House, where the last Scottish parliament was held in 1707.
The Castle, where you can see the Crown Jewels worn by the Kings and Queens of Scotland.

46

UNIT 8

Nearly late for Work

This story happened in 1822 in Dundee

"Wake up, John! I hear them moving in the street. It must be near five o'clock. You'll be late for work!"

Seven-year-old John Bell yawned sleepily, and opened his eyes to look at his mother as she stood by his bedside. How tired she looked! The family had no clock. She was always frightened that they might sleep in, so she sat up half the night after she got home from work at ten o'clock.

"I'm away to the mill now," she said as she wrapped her shawl round herself and the baby. "There's a bit bread there on the table for your dinner."

John jumped up quickly. The Dens Spinning Mill where he worked started at 5.30 am. If he was late for work he would lose his wages and the foreman might beat him. He might even lose his job!

He shut the door of the single-roomed house, and went quickly down the narrow stairs into Bucklemakers Wynd. A coal seller's cart stood outside the close. "Maybe we'll get a wee drop coal on Saturday when I get my pay," he thought.

Two men pushed past, nearly knocking him down.

"The mill clock says half-past five," said one. "They've put it on fast again!"

John began to run as fast as he could. The crowds were pushing through the mill gates as the clock struck the half-hour. Slowly the gates began to close. Quickly John slid through the narrow opening and heard the gate clang shut behind him. He was in time!

These children are working in a spinning factory

In the early nineteenth century, children often worked for very long hours in factories which spun and wove cloth.

Factory owners could pay children much less than grown-ups. Children were small enough to crawl under the machines to keep them clean. Sometimes children started work when they were only five or six years old. They often worked the same hours as adults. Mothers had to take their babies and young children to work, if there was no one to look after them at home.

John worked six days a week in 1822. Here is a time-table of his working day.

5 am	get up
5.30 am	start work
8 am	stop for breakfast
8.30 am	back to work
2 pm	stop for dinner
2.30 pm	back to work
7 pm	stop work

In the busy time work might not stop until 10 pm

1. How long was his working day?
2. How long did he get for meals?
3. How many hours a week did he go to work?
4. Did John go to school?
5. When might John have time to play?
6. a. How many hours would John have free from Saturday night till Monday morning?
   b. How many hours do you have free from Friday evening till Monday morning?
7. Make a list of the times at which you get up, go to school, have meals, play. How long do you spend working in a week?

Sometimes John worked longer hours. Mill owners quite often put the clocks forward in the mornings and back at night. That meant their workers would start early and finish late. Very few workers owned a clock or a watch.

8. Why might a mill owner put up a notice like this?

BROWN'S MILL

Any worker found with a watch will be dismissed

By Order

John and the other factory children were small for their age compared to children living in the country side. They looked thin and pale.

9. Can you suggest why this might be? Think of all the things which help to keep you well and strong – good food, fresh air, exercise, plenty of sleep.

John found it hard to keep awake because he was often tired and hungry. Sometimes he was slow at his work. He had to stand for so long that his feet and legs became swollen. One day, the foreman found him yawning, and beat him hard with a cane.

10. Do you think John would work harder in the morning or afternoon?
    Say why.
11. Why would John keep on working for such long hours in a mill where he was beaten and ill-treated?

Working at a spinning machine. You can see a boy crawling under the machine

John's family needed the money which he earned. His father was dead, and his mother could not earn enough for all of them. Here is a list of wages for a mill in Dundee.

12. How much would John earn?
13. How much would his mother earn?
14. Every week they paid 1s.(5p) for rent. How much was left to live on?
15. What else would they need to spend money on?
16. Accidents could easily happen in a mill like this. Point out some of the dangers for workers.

Children under 7 working only 68 hours per week	1s. 8d. weekly	8p
Children over 7 working 76 hours	3s. weekly	15p
Women working 76 hours as spinners	7s. weekly	35p
Men working 76 hours as weavers	12s. weekly	60p

The newspapers in Dundee usually printed news of the worst accidents in the mills.

17. What happened to this young woman?
18. Would she find it easy to work in a mill afterwards?
19. What could the factory owner have done to try to stop accidents like this?

On Tuesday last, a young woman got one of her arms caught up in the rollers of her machine. She was taken to hospital where the badly cut arm was removed.

Not all mills were bad places to work. The mills at New Lanark were owned by Robert Owen. He had a shop which sold goods and cheap food to his workers. He built good houses for them and charged a fair rent. No children under ten worked in his factory. The younger children of his workers went to a school which he started.

Robert Owen's school at New Lanark

When children from other factories were given lessons after work, the teachers said it was very hard to teach them anything. They often fell asleep.

20. What are the children in the top picture doing?
21. What other lessons might the children have?

22. Why do you think there are visitors watching the children?
23. Do you think children would fall asleep at Robert Owen's school?

Many people wanted to make life better for workers. Parliament sent out inspectors to look at the factories and ask people about their work.

By the end of the nineteenth century people did not have to work such long hours. Young children like John were able to go to school and have time to play.

A factory inspector at work

Things to Do

Writing

1. You are a factory inspector who has been to a Dundee spinning mill. Describe what you saw, heard and smelt when you visited the mill without warning at six o'clock yesterday evening.
2. Here is a song about the children who worked in the mills.

My mother rises out o' bed   The sadness fills her gentle heart
She wakens in the gloom   When she to me does say
Turns me out in the morning   "I never thought to have you work
Then works her lonely loom   For fourpence a day."

You might like to try writing your own song about the mill children.

Acting

Read this carefully and act out with other people in the class what happens next.

John Bell is working at his machine. He feels the scarf round his neck growing tight. It is caught in the machine. He is dragged towards the moving machinery, and bangs his head badly. Another boy manages to pull him free. He sits down to recover and falls asleep. The mill foreman finds him. . . .

Places to Visit

1. It might be possible for your class to visit a modern factory or speak to someone who works in a factory. Think of the questions you might like to ask.
2. Sometimes old mills have been altered so that people can live in them. e.g. Dean Village, Edinburgh. Do you know of any buildings like this which are now used for something else?
3. A number of museums have displays of older factory tools. e.g. People's Palace, Glasgow, Gladstone Court Museum, Biggar.

Books to Read

Children of the Industrial Revolution by P. Davies (Wayland, 1972).
Shaftesbury and the Working Children by J. L. Davies (Jackdaw, 1964).
Victorian Children by E. Allen (*Junior Reference Books*, A. & C. Black, 1973).

UNIT 9

Heave awa' Hoose

This story happened in Edinburgh in November, 1861

It had been a cold, windy day in Edinburgh. Most people who lived in the High Street would normally have been glad to sit by the fire to keep warm. Instead they stood quietly huddled together looking at the pile of rubble which had once been a building six storeys high.

Men with pickaxes and shovels were working frantically to clear away some of the stones and dirt. 78 people were known to have lived there, and so far only 42 had been brought out alive.

A woman with her face streaked with dirt was crying bitterly. Her two children were missing. An old man, with cuts on his hands and face, looked sadly at the ruin. He had lived there all his life.

"There can't be anyone left alive there now," said a man at the front of the crowd. "It's a long time since it fell down."

Suddenly there was a shout from one of the rescuers. "There's someone here! I can hear him speaking!"

A hush fell on the crowd as the man began to tug at a large beam of wood sticking up from the rubble. A voice, faint but cheerful, could be heard.

"Heave awa' chaps. I'm no deid yet!"

The person who shouted "Heave awa'!" was a twelve-year-old boy called Joseph McIver. He was trapped by the legs and quite badly hurt, but still he kept calling out to his rescuers. A great cheer went up from the crowd when he was brought out safely. Later, when another house was built at the same place at 101 High Street, it was called "Heave-Awa' Hoose". This house is still there today.

1. What does it say above the entrance to the building?
2. Whose head is carved above the doorway?

Many of the big towns in Scotland, like Glasgow, Edinburgh and Dundee, had houses which were very old, damp and unpleasant to live in. New factories opened up, and many people crowded into the towns to work, but not enough good new houses were built. In large *tenements* (blocks of flats), built near the factories, whole families might live in a single room.

This picture of the rescue appeared in *The Illustrated London News,* one of the news magazines of the time

54

Sometimes as many as 15 people lived in one of these rooms. Some of them were just like cellars. They did not even have a window. There was only an open fire or a small range to cook on. Often there was no water inside the house. It had to be carried from a pump outside. Everyone who lived in the same block of houses used the same lavatory, which was often dirty and unhealthy.

3. How would food be cooked for these families?
4. Why would it take longer to cook then than it does now?
5. Where would the people get the water needed for cooking, washing dishes or washing clothes?
6. Could many clothes be dried at the same time?
7. Why would it be difficult to keep the houses clean?
8. When workers came home tired and dirty from their day's work, how long do you think it would take them to wash themselves?
9. In what ways might you find these houses unpleasant to live in?

Nineteenth-century
tenements in Glasgow

People were often sick in these damp, cold, dirty houses, which were crowded together. Many children were very ill with diseases such as typhus, diphtheria and scarlet fever. People often got drunk because life was so miserable and they wanted to forget their worries.

A headmaster wrote this in his school record book in 1873.

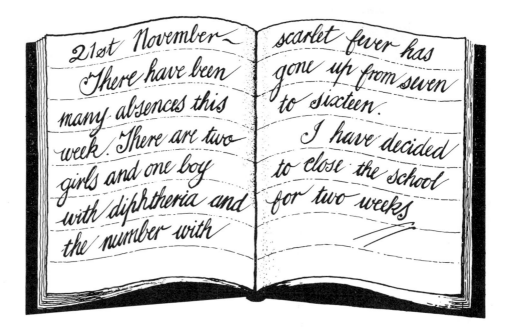

> 21st November—
> There have been many absences this week. There are two girls and one boy with diphtheria and the number with scarlet fever has gone up from seven to sixteen.
> I have decided to close the school for two weeks

10. How many children were absent with scarlet fever?
11. What had the headmaster decided to do?
12. Why do you think so many children were ill at one time?
13. Why do few children catch these diseases today?

The terrible accident to Joseph McIver's home shocked many of the richer people. They did not know how bad some of the houses in Edinburgh really were in 1861. Better houses began to be built for workers, and bad old houses were knocked down. But even today there are still places in Scotland where more new houses need to be built quickly.

Things to Do

Writing

1. Some details are missing from this story of the accident. Write out the paragraph and put in the missing words.

   A serious accident happened in Edinburgh in the month of . . . A tenement building of . . . storeys fell down in the . . . Street. Only forty-three people were rescued alive although . . . had lived in the building. One boy called . . . McIver was found when he called out that he was still alive.

2. Imagine you are Joseph McIver being interviewed by a newspaper reporter. Tell the story of the accident.
3. You have been asked to look at some of the workers' houses in Glasgow in 1860, and make a report about them. Write down what you might say.

Drawing and Painting

Draw a picture-strip to show:

1. Joseph McIver in his home when he hears a loud cracking noise.
2. People rushing to see the building which has fallen down.
3. People trying to help those who are trapped.
4. Joseph McIver shouting for help.
5. Everyone cheering when Joseph is saved.

Write underneath each picture what is happening.

Acting

A one-roomed house in Edinburgh or Glasgow in the nineteenth century might have been about 4.25 m × 3 m. Mark out a space this size in the classroom. Now mark out places for the door, the window, the fireplace, a cupboard, a chest for clothes, a table, two chairs and one bed.

Choose 8 people to be the family who live in this house. There is a father, mother, 3 boys, 2 girls and a baby. Find places to sit in the house during the day.

Act out what happens when:

1. Mother does the washing. How does she hang it out?
2. The children want to play marbles. Is there enough room? What does Mother say?
3. It is tea-time. Mother needs water. Who fetches it? How does she

heat the kettle? Father comes home from work. The baby is crying. Where does everyone sit to have tea?

4. It starts to rain. Mother takes in the washing through the window. Where do the wet clothes go? What will happen as you walk about the room?

5. Father wants to go out. He washes his hands and face. Mother wants to wash the baby. There is no water left. What happens?

6. It is bed-time. Find places to sleep. You might have to keep a mattress under the bed during the day and bring it out at night. Perhaps someone could sleep under the table. Several people will have to sleep in the same bed. Small children might sleep across the bed at the foot.

Places to Visit

1. In Edinburgh you can still see "Heave-Awa' Hoose" at 101 High Street. In other towns there may still be some old tenement houses near you. Do they have narrow entrance closes? How big are the windows? Is there perhaps an old wash-house in the back court?

2. Many museums now have displays which show the kinds of houses people lived in during the nineteenth century. Perhaps there is one in a museum near you.

Something to Talk About

"It is easier now for most people to keep their houses clean and comfortable than it was in the nineteenth century." Do you think this is true? Say why.

Books to Read

These books will tell you more about life in the towns in the nineteenth century:

The Victorians (*Picture Reference Books*, Brockhampton, 1967)
Victorian Times by V. Bailey and E. Wise (Longman, 1972)
Victorian Children by E. Allen (*Junior Reference Books*, A. & C. Black, 1973).

UNIT 10

No School Holiday

This story happened in a school in Huntly, Aberdeenshire in 1880

Mr McFie, the schoolmaster, looked sharply round the class as he came in. There was complete silence. All the pupils stood at their desks waiting for the order to sit down. Wee Jeanie McGregor in the front row rubbed her bare feet together nervously. George Ogilvie, the farmer's son, stood smiling confidently.

"Take your hands out of your pockets," Mr McFie thundered looking at the tawse which hung on the wall, "or I'll warm them in a way you won't forget!"

He walked over to his desk. There, lying right in the centre, lay three ripe stalks of barley. Slowly, Mr McFie picked them up and dropped them in the wastepaper basket. He picked up his pointer and gave Willie Duncan a sharp dig in the ribs, saying "Wake up boy! This is not a school holiday. There's work to be done."

The class groaned, but Mr McFie kept them all hard at work. The sun streamed through the window as they wrote, squeakily, on their slates.

In the afternoon the inkwells were filled, pens and pen-wipers were given out and everyone practised writing in books.

At last, at half-past three, the last writing book was handed in. The teacher sat in his high chair, looked sternly at the class and said, "The school will be closed for the harvest for the next five weeks."

"Hooray!" shouted George. "Three cheers for our dominie, Mr McFie! Three cheers for the holidays!"

With a beaming smile, Mr McFie lifted the large brass bell and rang it loudly. The holidays had begun.

A hundred years ago teachers were often very strict with their pupils. Classes were large and sometimes a teacher taught pupils of all ages. Each class was called a *standard*.

The headmaster decided when it was time to give holidays. Often schools stayed open on Christmas Day!

Children were glad of the chance to earn money by working in the fields at harvest time.

The picture shows a class in 1890. Look at the gas lights hanging from the ceiling.

1. How many pupils are in the class?
2. How many pupils sit at each desk?
3. Would it be easy to move these desks?
4. Do the boys and girls sit together?
5. What do you notice about the floor of the classroom?
6. Why would it not be easy for these children to look out of the window?
7. What are the children doing?

The teacher who is taking the lesson is a pupil teacher. She is learning how to teach. The class teacher stands at the back of the room.

The children probably looked forward to lessons like this one. Most of the time was spent doing reading, writing and arithmetic. Usually the children wrote on slates with a special slate pencil. They carried a little tin with a wet sponge to clean the slates.

Every day the children practised multiplication tables and mental arithmetic.

Here is a Test Card Mr McFie gave his class.

8. Is it like the arithmetic you do? Does it look easy or hard?

9. 2d was worth less than one penny (1p). What do you notice about the price of rolls over 100 years ago?

10. Would it cost people as much to buy their food as it does today?

11. Why do you think children then would be very pleased to be given 3d (about 1p) to spend?

STANDARD V.—CARD 24.

1. If 16 men take 8 weeks to finish a piece of work, working 10 hours a day, how long will 20 men take to finish it?

2. Find the value of 9005 articles, at 14s. $7\frac{1}{4}$d. each.

3. Simplify $(2\frac{1}{2} + 3\frac{1}{4}) \div (3\frac{1}{4} - 2\frac{1}{2})$.

4. Make out and receipt the following bill:
   2 cwts. 1 qr. of sugar, at 2d. per lb.
   96 lbs. of tea,   at 1/5$\frac{1}{2}$ per lb.
   380 rolls,   at 5 for 2d.
   17$\frac{1}{4}$ lbs. of tea,   at 2/6 per lb.

There were special rules for writing lessons. Children were not allowed to write with the left hand. Mr McFie punished Willie Duncan for doing this.

12. Which hand do you write with? Try holding your pencil as the rules say.

1. **Sit up straight.**
2. **Put your left hand on the desk.**
3. **Hold pen with right hand. Put your forefinger on top of the pen, your second finder at the side and bend your thumb underneath.**
4. **Have the palm of your hand facing the paper.**
5. **Point your pen to the right.**

13. When it was time for the reading lesson, the whole class turned to the correct page. Each person in turn read part of the story. Sometimes it took over two hours to give everyone a chance to read.

Do you think this would be an interesting lesson?

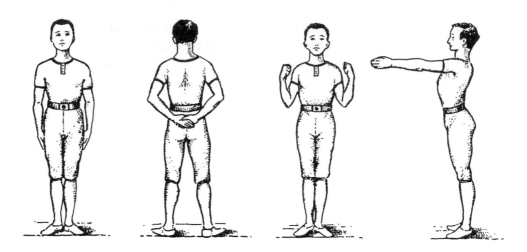

Every week Mr Baxter, the drill sergeant, came. He had been in the army for many years. The boys and girls lined up in the playground, and he drilled them just as he had drilled soldiers in the army. They learned to march in step, change step and mark time. Poor wee Jeannie McGregor hated this, for she always turned left instead of right, and Mr Baxter got very cross.

There were exercises, too, like the ones shown in the top picture. They are taken from a book made for schools in 1904.

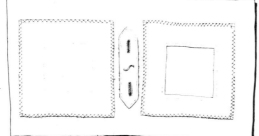

All the girls had knitting and sewing lessons from Miss Taylor, the infant teacher.

They might make a sampler like the one shown here.

By the time they were 11, they could do work like that shown at the bottom of the page.

14. What was the name of the girl who sewed the sampler?
15. Which class was she in?
16. When did she make it?
17. The bottom drawing shows how to make a neat patch on a piece of material. What else does it show?

Every Monday morning the teacher asked pupils their Catechism.
This was a long list of questions and answers about religion.
Everyone had to know the correct answer or they might be punished.

THE PROOF CATECHISM.

WITH PARAPHRASES, NOTES, AND ANALYSIS.

1. *What is the chief end of man?*
Man's chief end is to glorify God, and *to enjoy him* for ever.

Man's chief end is to glorify God.—1 Cor. 10.31. Whether therefore ye eat, or drink, or whatsoever ye do, do all to the glory of God.

Man's chief end is to enjoy God for ever.—Ps. 73. 25, 26. Whom have I in heaven but thee? And there is none upon earth that I desire besides thee. My flesh and my heart faileth; but God is the strength of my heart, and my portion for ever.

2. *What rule hath God given to direct us how we may glorify and enjoy him?*

The *Word of God,* which is contained in the *Scriptures* of the Old and New Testaments, is the only *rule* to *direct us* how we may glorify and enjoy him.

Once a year the Inspector came to see if pupils were good enough to pass on to the next class. Mr McFie made sure that every pupil did his very best. They recited the tables over and over again, until even little Jeannie knew them by heart. They learned long lists of dates for history, and knew the name of every mountain, river, cape and bay in Scotland.

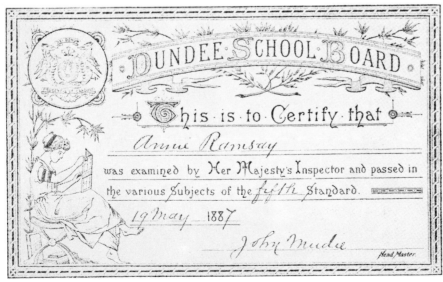

Everyone who passed got a certificate.

18. Where did this girl go to school?   19. Which class was she in?

The school was hard work, but at playtime and after school children played lots of games.

The girls liked singing or skipping games such as "Ring o' Roses", "Queen Mary", "I came to see Jemima" or "Babbity Bowster".

Boys often had a gird and cleek and ran noisy races up and down the road. Marbles was another favourite, and most boys and girls had a wooden spinning top or peerie.

20. What games are the children shown on this page playing?

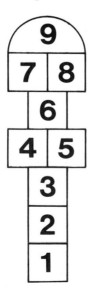

Sometimes they marked out a shape on the pavement with chalk, and played peever with an old flat tin.

21. Look at the diagram. Have you ever played this game? What is your name for it?

No wonder they all looked forward to the holidays. They might not have many toys, but they could still have lots of fun.

Things to Do

Writing

1. Tell this story in your own words and give it an ending: The inspector has come to visit the school. He is a small man with a large nose. He gives the class an arithmetic test. He walks up and down. A boy at the back tries to cover his paper. The inspector snatches it and sees a drawing of someone with an enormous nose. . . .
2. Write down the words of any singing or skipping games you know. Draw pictures of them and make a wall chart.

Drawing and Painting

Draw and paint pictures to show:

1. Mr McFie ringing the school bell.
2. Children a hundred years ago playing a game.

Acting

Read this carefully and act out with other people in the class what happens next. The class are having a writing lesson. Books and pens are given out. One boy is asked to put ink in the inkwells. As he carries the bottle up to the back of the room, another boy sticks out his foot to trip him up.

Something to Talk About

Would you have liked to go to school in the nineteenth century?

People and Places to Visit

1. If your school is an old one, look for signs of what school was once like. Are there any old desks with holes for inkwells? Does the school have an old blackboard with lines for writing? Is there an old school bell?
2. Ask older people, like grandparents, what school was like when they were young, and what games they played.
3. One very interesting place where you can find out about the toys children played with is the Museum of Childhood in Edinburgh. Your local Museum may have some toys and games too.

Books to Read

Your teacher might read you more about school life in the nineteenth century from *Learning and Teaching in Victorian Times* by P. F. Speed (Longman, 1964).

UNIT 11

Maggie the Housemaid

This story happened in Gourock in 1909

The porter at Gourock station lifted down Maggie's box and put it on the platform. She felt very lonely. That morning Maggie had said goodbye to her family and travelled in a train for the first time in her life.

A man stood near her. He was very smartly dressed in a dark blue suit with gold buttons and black leather gaiters. "I'm Colonel Simpson's driver – or *chauffeur* to the master. Are you the new housemaid for Craigton House?" he said in a gruff voice.

"Yes Sir," said Maggie.

The man picked up her box and she followed him out of the station. There stood a real motor car! Maggie stared at the shiny red monster with its big brass lamps and horn. She had only seen a car once before when it went roaring through the village at home.

An hour later they turned into the driveway of a large mansion house.

"Here we are," said the chauffeur. "I'll take you round to the servants' entrance. The housekeeper's expecting you."

He knocked at a door and led Maggie inside.

"Mrs McKenzie!" he called.

A stout red-faced woman came forward. "So this is Maggie," she said. "Turn round and let me look at you. Well, you look neat and willing, but you've a lot to learn before you can be a good servant in a gentleman's household. I'll expect you to work hard, Maggie. Now, come with me and I'll take you to see the mistress."

Maggie was fourteen when she began work in Colonel Simpson's house. She was paid £20 a year. At home in Ayrshire she had shared a bedroom with her four sisters, but at Craigton House she had a tiny bedroom all to herself. It was up in the attic, at the top of the house. She was so tired after all the excitement of her journey that she fell asleep as soon as she went to bed.

Next morning, she was wakened by a loud knock at half-past five. She washed her hands and face in the basin of cold water on the washstand, and then dressed carefully in her new grey housemaid's dress, working apron and cap. She hurried down the back stairs to the kitchen.

1. Why would Maggie have to get up so early?
2. What time do you get up in the morning?

Turn over the page. You will see that Maggie had a lot to do before she served breakfast.

The housekeeper explained to Maggie what she must do every day. Here is a list of her duties.

THE DUTIES OF THE HOUSEMAID

Before family have breakfast

1. Open the window shutters in the diningroom, drawing room, breakfast room and library.
2. Take out the hearth rugs and shake them.
3. Sweep out the breakfast room.
4. Clean out all the fires, black-lead and polish the grates.
5. Light the fires.
6. Dust and polish furniture carefully.
7. Sweep down the stairs.
8. Wash the front door step.
9. Polish the front door handle, and letter box.
10. Wash hands carefully and put on a clean apron.
11. Lay the breakfast table.

---

3. Why do you think shutters were closed over the windows at night?
4. Why do people not light fires in every room today?
5. Do you have a coal fire in your house?
6. In what other ways can houses be heated?

Maggie had to use brushes like these to sweep out the rooms.

Every room had a washstand with a large jug and basin. Maggie had to carry hot water up from the basement to the bedrooms on the upper floors.

7. What would probably be used for sweeping rooms today?
8. Would carrying hot water upstairs from the basement be easy? What would it be carried in?
9. What other things would Maggie have to carry upstairs?
10. Why do you think Maggie had to wash and put on a clean apron before she set the breakfast table?

When the family breakfast was over, there was more work. The bedrooms had to be cleaned and polished. The mattresses on the beds were turned over every day, so that they would not be lumpy and uncomfortable.

At lunch-time Maggie helped to serve the meal. She was so frightened that she nearly spilt the soup, but Mrs Simpson smiled kindly, and told her she was managing very well.

SERVING AT TABLE

Always look neat and clean.

Serve on the left hand of the person you are serving.

Move quietly.

Never speak unless asked. A good servant should not be noticed.

Maggie serving at dinner in the evening

The servants had their lunch in the huge kitchen down in the basement. As soon as she was finished, Maggie had to hurry upstairs to change into her good black dress and cap and apron trimmed with white lace.

When Maggie came downstairs again, Mrs McKenzie looked at her very carefully. "We can't have you answering the front door to callers with your cap on one side. Now you sit and help me mend the sheets and pillow-cases, and whenever the door bell rings you must answer it. At 4 o'clock you will serve afternoon tea."

HOW TO ANSWER THE DOOR

1. **Greet the caller by saying "Good morning" or "Good afternoon, Sir" (or "Madam").**
2. **When the caller asks for a member of the family say, "I'll see if Mrs . . . is at home. Whom shall I say is calling?"**
3. **When you return say, "Mrs . . . is in the drawing room. Come this way, Sir" (or "Madam").**
4. **At the door knock and announce the caller saying, "Mrs . . . to see you, Madam."**

---

11. If Maggie answers the door to someone, what should she say to them?

In the evening Maggie would lay the dining room table, light the bedroom fires and help to serve dinner. She usually went to bed about 10 o'clock.

Sometimes Maggie thought how nice it would be to take the place of Colonel Simpson's daughter, Clara, just for a day. She could lie in bed until half-past eight in the morning, and in the afternoon she could go calling at other fine houses and have afternoon tea.

"How lovely it would be," she thought. "But I'm just a servant."

A group of servants who worked in a bigger house than Colonel Simpson's

Things to Do

Writing

1. Life at Craigton House was very different from the village Maggie came from. Write the letter Maggie might send home to her family telling them about her first week at work.

2. Today we have a great number of gadgets and machines which make housework much easier. Make a list of all the things which help with washing, cleaning, cooking and storing.

Drawing and Painting

1. At Craigton House there was a housekeeper, a cook, a kitchenmaid, a lady's maid, a chauffeur, a gardener and a gardener's boy as well as Maggie. Draw a picture of them all in the kitchen.

2. If you can find a book on early motor cars at the library you could make a picture frieze. Each person could draw a different car. Then paste them all on a long strip of paper.

Acting

1. Think of all the jobs Maggie had to do. Without speaking, act out one of these jobs in front of the class and see if the others can guess what you are doing.

2. A number of people should act as visitors who have come to call on Mrs Simpson. One person acts as Maggie who answers the door and shows them into the drawing room.

3. Make a class play. Colonel Simpson is giving an important dinner party. The family and guests hear the gong, leave the drawing room and take their places at the dinner table. Colonel Simpson sits at the head of the table, his wife at the foot. Maggie is helping to serve. Outside the dining room Mrs McKenzie had scolded her for looking untidy. She carries in the dish of roast mutton, trips on the carpet and drops the mutton on the floor.
What happens next?

Making Models

Copy the shape of a suitable figure from a magazine, paste it onto a piece of stiff cardboard, and cut it out. Make a stand at the back. Draw and cut out clothes for Maggie. Remember to make tabs so that the clothes can fit on the model. Different people in the class could dress models for Colonel and Mrs Simpson, Clara and all the servants.

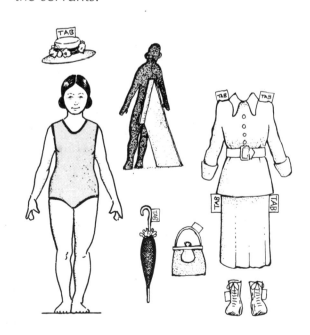

Something to Talk About
1. Maggie probably enjoyed her new job. Do you think this is true?
2. People don't really need servants nowadays. Do you agree?

Finding Out
Although Maggie was only paid £20 a year, things cost much less then than they do now. Look at this list of 1909 prices. See if you can find out how much it would cost to buy the same things today.

Cake tin	9d.	(4p)	Tin opener	6d.	(2$\frac{1}{2}$p)
Dust pan	1s.	(5p)	Pail	1s.	(5p)
Iron kettle	3s.	(15p)	Frying pan	1s. 4d.	(7p)
Saucepan	1s. 6d.	(7$\frac{1}{2}$p)	Sweeping brush	2s. 6d.	(12$\frac{1}{2}$p)
Coffee pot	2s.	(10p)	Margarine – 1 lb	6d.	(2$\frac{1}{2}$p)

Places to Visit
1. In most districts there is a historic house which is open to the public at certain times. Perhaps the class could visit it. Try to work out the numbers of rooms, where the cooking would be done, where the servants would live and what kind of work the servants would have to do if there were no modern gadgets to help them.
2. The Georgian House, Charlotte Square, Edinburgh has a fine kitchen in the basement. Other examples of kitchens are at Drumlanrig in Dumfriesshire, Inveraray Castle in Argyllshire and Kellie Castle near Pittenweem. If you live near the Border you might be able to visit the kitchen at Wallington, Northumberland.
3. You may be able to see the kind of car which took Maggie to Craigton House in a transport museum.
4. Your local library will have books about houses, transport, costume and entertainment. Look at them to find out more about life at this time.

Books to Read
Two good stories about a young girl who works as a maid are:

An Hour in the Morning by G. Cooper (Oxford University Press, 1971) and A Time in a City by G. Cooper (Oxford University Press, 1972).
Kitchens and Cooking by K. and M. Eldon (Wayland) describes the kind of kitchen Maggie worked in.

UNIT 12

Billy Leaves Home

This story happened in 1939 when Great Britain was at war

Billy Moffat stood on the platform of Partick station in Glasgow one Saturday morning in September. He was trying to look cheerful and happy. The station was full of children from Billy's school.

A train steamed into the station. Billy had only been on a train once before, when he went to Largs on holiday. Some of his friends had never been on a train at all. A porter rushed up opening the doors of each carriage. The children piled in. A whistle blew and the train chugged slowly out of the station. They were off!

It seemed a very long time before the train stopped again. It was two o'clock when they reached Kippen. Everyone stared round about. It was not at all like noisy, dirty Partick. There were fields everywhere.

It was very hot walking down the road and Billy grew tired of carrying his case and gas mask. He felt very hungry. They went into a school playground, and formed a long line.

A group of people who had been standing at the school gate began to walk down the line. A fat, pleasant-looking lady stopped in front of Billy. She looked at the label pinned to his jacket. "Billy Moffat," she read. "Right Billy, come with me. I'm Mrs Grant."

Feeling very shy, Billy lifted his case again and followed the fat lady to his new home.

Adolf Hitler, the leader of Germany, had strong armies. He used them to take over other countries round about. (Czechoslovakia, Austria and Poland.) In September 1939 Great Britain went to war to stop Hitler. The war lasted six years.

People were afraid the Germans might use bombers to attack big cities like Glasgow, Edinburgh or Dundee. School children were sent away to the country to be safe. They were called evacuees.

The top picture shows a street in Clydebank near Glasgow after a bombing raid.

In case the Germans used poison gas, everyone was given a gasmask.

1. Choose a good word to end this sentence.
   Evacuees had to leave home to go to a place where they would be . . .
2. Look at the second picture. What do you think the nurse is telling the children?
3. Why are the children in the third picture carrying cases?
4. What is in the cardboard boxes everyone carries?
5. What kind of train is it?
6. How can you tell that there is no corridor on this train?

Gas mask practice

Billy could only take one case with him.

7. Try to unscramble the letters to find out what was in it.
8. Suggest other things he might need.
9. Sometimes girls took a doll or a teddy bear with them. What would you have taken?
10. Billy had to wear the label on his jacket. Why do you think the children all had labels like this?

At first Billy found life strange in Kippen.

11. If he looked out of the window in Glasgow what would he see?
12. What would he see in the country?

So that enemy planes could not see where to bomb, no one could show a light after dark. Billy's mother put up black-out curtains.

13. Why would it be hard for Billy's mother and father to go out (visiting) at night?

There was just enough food to go round. To share it out fairly everyone was given a ration book. When you bought food the shopkeeper marked the book so that you could not buy any more of that kind of food that week. This is what Billy was allowed for one week.

14. What foods can you see?
15. Do you eat more than this in one week?

Other foods were not easy to get.

16. Try to fill in the missing letters to find some of the scarce foods.

SW—ET—
RA—S—NS
BI—CU—TS
OR—NG—S

8oz Fat
2oz Tea
2 slices Cooked Meat
4oz Ham
1oz Cheese
8oz Sugar
2oz Jam
1s. worth of Meat
1 Egg

There were no bananas for sale. When a five-year-old girl was given a banana at the end of the war, she tried to eat it with the skin on.

17. Why would she do this?

Billy did not have many clothes. To buy new clothes you had to have clothing coupons.

Billy only had enough coupons for shoes and a raincoat. Mrs Grant used her husband's old suit to make Billy two new pairs of trousers. She unpicked two old woollen scarves and knitted him a striped jumper.

Clothing coupons

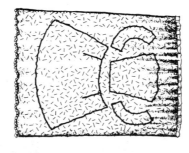

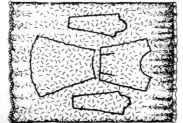

18. What do you think she made for herself from this pair of curtains?

Billy's father joined the army. He was in the Gordon Highlanders and fought in France and later in Egypt. For three years Billy did not see him. He was very proud when his father won a medal for bravery.

At home in Glasgow, Billy's mother worked in the Rolls Royce factory making aeroplane parts. It was not easy for her to visit Billy very often.

19. Billy sometimes worried about what might happen to his father. Why?
20. At Kippen Billy always rushed to meet the postman. Who would he hope had sent him a letter?
21. Billy was eight when the war started in 1939. How old would he be when it ended in 1945?

Billy went home to White Street. On 8th May there there was a big party in the street to celebrate the end of the war. Everyone brought food for the party. There was singing and dancing. At the end of the street the boys lit a big bonfire.

"I'm glad to be home again," Billy said to himself.

A street party in Dundee to celebrate the end of the war

Things to Do

Writing

1. You are an evacuee like Billy. Write a letter to your friend who has stayed at home about your life in the country.
2. Here are two poems written by children about life during the Second World War. Write a poem about being an evacuee, an air raid, food in war-time or something else which interests you.

What I miss, I miss my mum
She's not here when I wake
I miss my school, I miss my fun
I miss the food my mum can bake.
There is no chip shop near me now
When I look out, I see a cow.

I'm down in the shelter
I hear the loud bang of the bombs
I'm frightened in case
We all lose our homes
My cat is outside
I wish it was down in
The shelter with me.

Something to Talk About

Would you have liked to live in wartime? Say why.

People to Ask

1. Ask older people to tell you of life in wartime. They could perhaps teach you one of the wartime songs such as "Run Rabbit Run" or "Roll out the Barrel".
2. Ask older people to help you make a class exhibition about the War. You could perhaps have medals, photographs, old newspapers, books and records as well as your own drawings, models and writing.

Places to Visit

There are still signs of the war to be found, such as the stumps of old iron railings which were removed to be made into aeroplanes, or old tank traps and gun sites near coasts. There are military museums at Edinburgh and Stirling Castles.

Books to Read

Look in the library for books about life in wartime such as *The Second World War* by Roy Rollock (*Signposts to History*, Macmillan).

   Some good stories are:

Carrie's War by Nina Bawden (Gollancz, 1973 and Heinemann, Educational, 1975)

We couldn't leave Dinah by Mary Treadgold (Cape, 1965)

Visitors from London by Kitty Barne (J. M. Dent, 1940)

Dawn of Fear by Susan Cooper (Chatto & Windus, 1972)

When Hitler Stole Pink Rabbit by Judith Kerr (Collins, 1971).

Information for the Teacher

Sources

The evidence upon which the stories in this book are based can be found chiefly in the following works:

V. Gordon Childe, *Ancient Dwellings at Skara Brae*, Edinburgh, HMSO, 1950.

A. O. & M. O. Anderson (ed.), *Adamnan's, Life of St Columba*, Nelson, 1961.

M. McDiarmid (ed.), *Hary's 'Wallace'*, Scottish Text Soc., 2 Vols., Blackwood, 1968.

Chronicle of Lanercost, trans. Sir Herbert Maxwell, MacLehose, 1913.

Chronicle of Walter of Guisborough, extracts trans. A. A. M. Duncan, Scottish Centre for Social Subjects, Glasgow.

The Statistical Account of Scotland, X.

E. Royston Pike, *Human Documents of the Industrial Revolution*, Allen & Unwin, 1966.

Diary of William Brown, 1819, Dundee University Ms. 15/26.

G. D. H. Cole, *The Life of Robert Owen*, Cass, 1965.

P. H. J. H. Gosden, *How they were taught*, Blackwood, 1969.

School Log Books, various.

Mrs Beeton, *Household Management*, Ward Lock, 1861 and later editions.

A. Calder, *The People's War*, Cape, 1969.

V. Massey, *The Child's war*, BBC, 1971.

For further Useful Material:

C. Thomas, *Britain and Ireland in Early Christian Times*, Thames & Hudson, 1971.

F. Marian McNeil, *Iona, A History of the Island*, Blackie, 1973.

Lucy Menzies, *St Columba of Iona*, Outram, 1970.

Andrew S. Cunningham, *Culross, Past and Present*, Purves and Cunningham, 1910.

Sir Walter Scott, *Tales of a Grandfather*, various editions.

Agnes Muir MacKenzie, *Scottish Pageant*, 4 vols, Oliver & Boyd, 1956–8.

F. R. Huggett, *Factory Life and Work*, Harrap, 1973.

I. & P. Opie, *Children and Games in Street and Playground*, Oxford University Press, 1969.

H. Hamilton, *History of the Homeland*, Allen & Unwin, 1947.

G. D. H. Cole and R. Postgate, *The Common People*, Methuen, 1949.

J. Warrack, *The Domestic Life of Scotland, 1488–1688*, Methuen, 1920.

W. Longmate, *How we lived then*, Hutchinson, 1971.

E. Barron, *The Scottish War of Independence*, Nisbet, 1914 (and later reprints).

A. D. Cameron, *History for Young Scots*, Books 1 & 2, Oliver & Boyd, 1963, 1980.

A. D. Cameron, *Living in Scotland 1760–1820*, Oliver & Boyd, 1969.

Then & There series, Longman, e.g.

W. Ritchie, *Scotland in the Days of Wallace and Bruce*

W. Ritchie, *Edinburgh in its Golden Age*

W. Stevenson, *Scotland in the Days of James IV*

H. Shapiro, *Scotland in the Days of James VI*

H. Shapiro, *Scotland in the Days of Burns*

N. Nichol, *Glasgow and the Tobacco Lords*.

Useful Reference Books:

A. A. M. Duncan, *Scotland, The Making of the Kingdom*, Oliver & Boyd, 1975, 1978.

R. Nicholson, *Scotland, The Later Middle Ages*, Oliver & Boyd, 1974, 1978.

G. Donaldson, *Scotland, James V to James VIII*, Oliver & Boyd, 1965, 1978.

W. Ferguson, *Scotland, 1689 to the present*, Oliver & Boyd 1968, 1978.

Classroom Activities
Useful advice will be found in:

J. Casciani & I. Watt, *Drama in the Primary School*, Nelson, 1966.

J. Deans, *Art and Craft in the Primary School*, Black, 1961.

J. A. Fairley, *Activity Methods in History*, Nelson, 1967.

J. A. Fairley, *Patch History and Creativity*, Longman, 1970.

M. Grater, *Make it in Paper*, Mills and Boon, 1961.

E. & E. Milliken, *Handwork Methods in the Teaching of History*, Wheaton, 1960.

A. Zaidenberg, *How to draw period costumes*, Abelard Schumann, 1966.

Useful Suppliers of Materials are

Airfix Products Ltd., Haldane Place, Garrat Lane, London, SW 18.

Britain's Models, 186 Kings Cross Road, London, WC1.

Dryad Handicrafts, Leicester.

Education Models, 4 Avenue Road, Duffield, Derbyshire.

Randall Page, 11 Old Bond Street, London, W1.

Revell Ltd., Maidstone House, Berners Street, London, W1.

Useful Addresses

Ancient Monument Publications, Department of the Environment, Argyle House, 3 Lady Lawson Street, Edinburgh, EH3 9SD.

Countryside Commission for Scotland, Battleby, Redgorton, Perth.

Forestry Commission, 231 Corstorphine Road, Edinburgh.

HM Stationery Office Bookshop, 13a Castle Street, Edinburgh.

Iona Community, 214 Clyde Street, Glasgow.

Landmark Visitors Centre, Stirling.

National Trust for Scotland, 5 Charlotte Square, Edinburgh.

New Lanark Conservation, The Counting House, New Lanark, Lanarkshire.

Royal Commission on Ancient and Historic Monuments of Scotland, 54 Melville Street, Edinburgh.

Scottish Record Office, Register House, Edinburgh.

Places to Visit
A selection of the more accessible local and national museums

The National Museum of Antiquities of Scotland and
The Scottish National Portrait Gallery, 1 Queen Street, Edinburgh.

The Royal Scottish Museum, Chambers Street, Edinburgh.

The Museum of Childhood, 38 High Street, Edinburgh.

Huntly House, 142 Canongate, Edinburgh.

Edinburgh Wax Museum, 142 High Street, Edinburgh.

Art Galleries and Museum, Kelvingrove, Dumbarton Road, Glasgow.